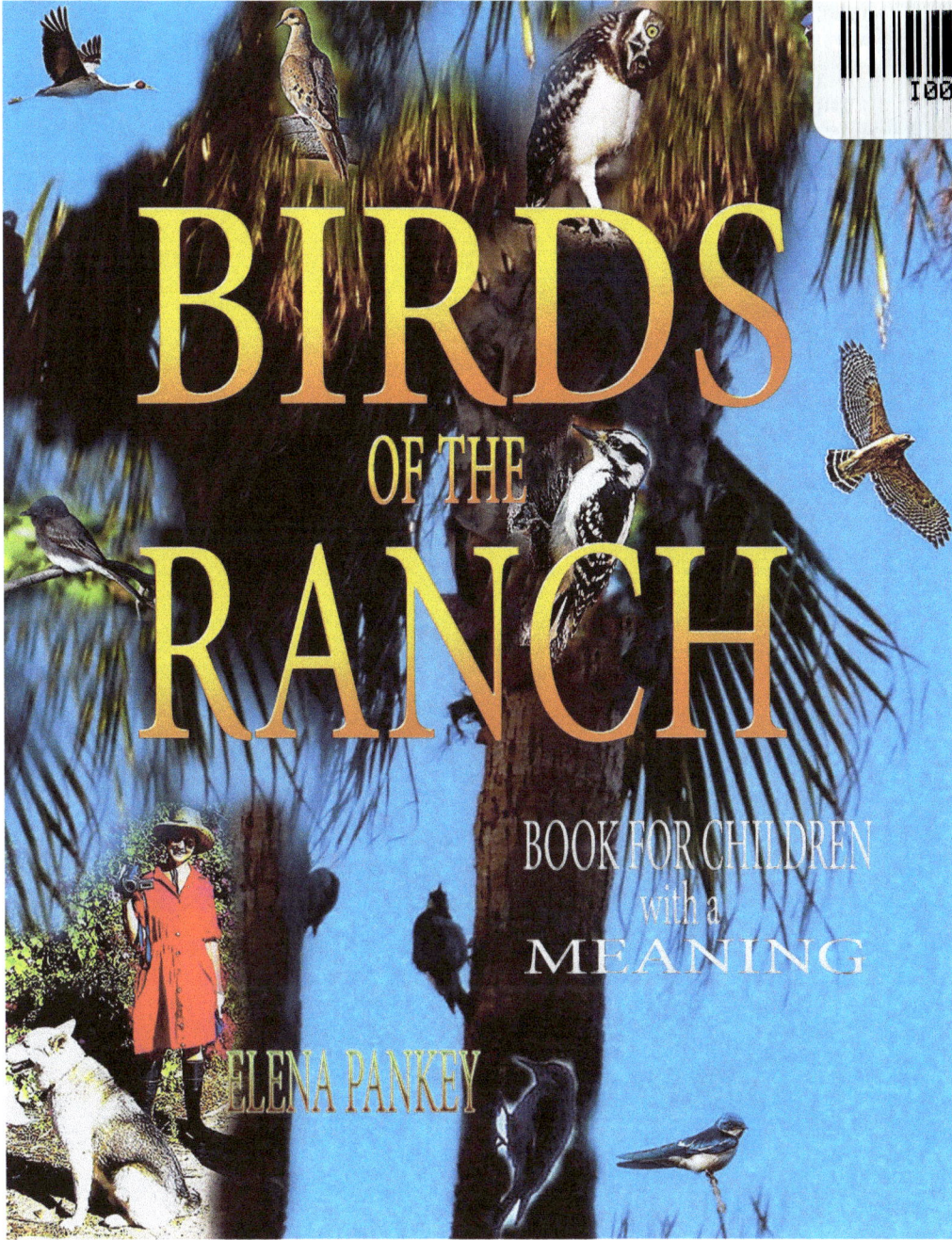

BIRDS
OF THE
RANCH

BOOK FOR CHILDREN
with a
MEANING

ELENA PANKEY

978-1-952907-50-0

Birds of the Ranch

Book for Children with a Meaning

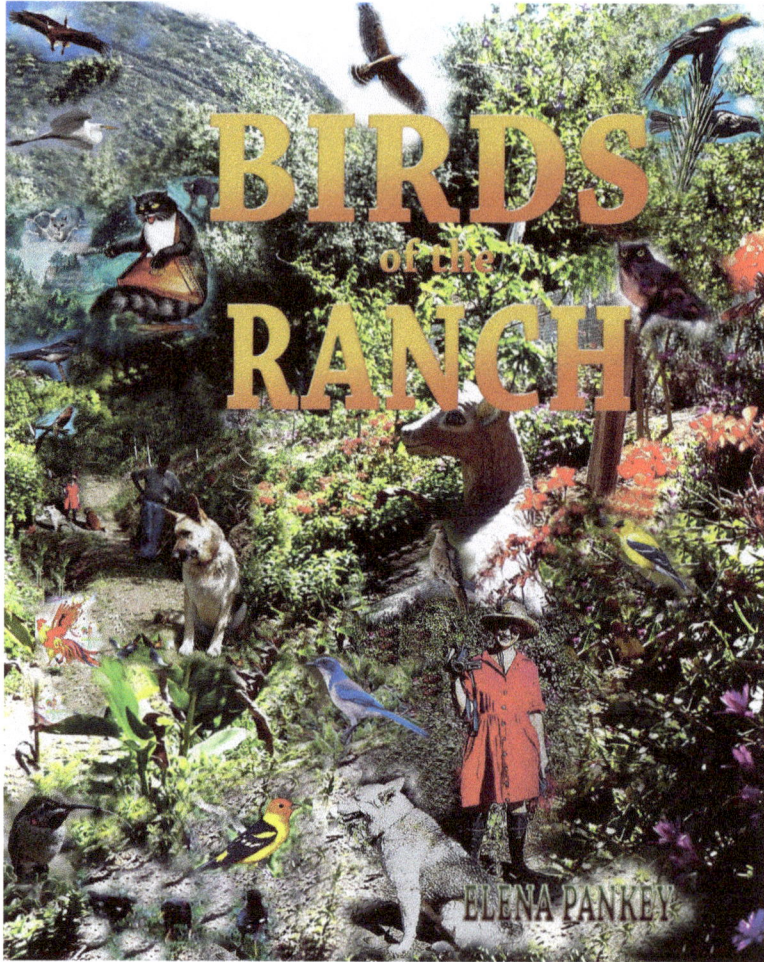

Elena Pankey

***

ISBN: : 978-1-952907-50-0

***

Contents

Introduction

This is a colorful book for children about some birds living on a California ranch. For many years the author and her dogs were observing the life of crows, hawks, owls, singing birds, trying to help all who needed their support. Some small singing birds were always courageously protecting their nests. A big Father-Bird was teaching his son to live independently. The most exciting story is about the loving parents of a young Owl, who were teaching their son to fly and got into a battle with a hawk.

The author often uses the form of a fairy tale, while talking about real events. The creative book cover and unique inner design are done by the author and are masterpieces.

Author

The author – Elena Pankey wrote many fascinating books in Russian and English languages, published in Europe and America. Among them, there are several funny books about cats and dogs, the monuments to these beloved animals are worth mentioning. Her books about Argentine tango or about a famous Ukrainian artist Valeria Bulat cannot be ignored. Memorial trilogy of her childhood town Gelendzik, people living there in 1950-1990 has historical value.

The author has many years of experience in various fields of education, literature, theater, dance, cinematography. She especially enjoyed working as a tour guide in the Leningrad palaces. During the years of "perestroika", she had her own successful business, which gave her the opportunity to travel the world. Finally, she found her true happiness in California, where she opened her dance school and produced many charity concerts.

Ranch

Once upon a time, there was an old ranch in South California. The avocado trees grew on the slopes of the warm hills, and the citrus plantation was down below in the valley. An owner's house located on the top of the hill. There was a shallow river running at the bottom of that hill.

Sometimes after the big rains, the river was coming out of the banks to flood the land, getting even to the citrus plantations. Sometimes around the river people could see the white cranes, elegantly flying from one spot to the other. In the spring, when more water was coming down from the mountains, a huge chorus of frogs cheerfully sang on the bottom of the river among the trees. The most beautiful time was during the spring when the citrus orchard was blooming and an incredible fragrance was filling the air.

Colorful Birds

Many colorful birds live on the Ranch, especially around the swimming pool, next to the house, where it is safer. They also live in the garden, as well, where they enjoy the fruit trees, bushes, and constant blooming flowers. In March a lot of singing birds come to the ranch. After short time looking around, they don't want to waste a day, and were looking for partners with whom it is fun to play their love games.

It is pleasant to wake up to the birds' songs. Before the sunrise, they are singing their beautiful songs of love and glorifying joyful life. Alenushka put several birds' houses in the garden and they occupied them right away. The garden was heaven for all living creatures.

Then in April the birds finally formed their families and began making their nests. The birds learned that their nests could be destroyed by crows and hawks. So they tried to build their homes in more protected locations, in the low part of the cypress or palm trees, closer to the front yard.

In May the singing birds were putting eggs in the nests and sat on them, waiting for the babies. Then, their small hungry chicks were yelling loudly, all the time asking for more food. When the mistress Alenushka was feeding her dogs, the bird's babies were asking her to help their parents to feed them.

Protecting Nests

In the spring many small birds usually were singing their greetings very close to the bedroom earlier in the morning. Then, several bold crows would come and loud stamps on the roof of the house. Alenushka was shooting towards the crow, trying to scare the big nasty birds away. This was how her days began.

It was amazing that in the spring when birds made their nests and fed their chicks, their friends were sitting high on the trees and looked out for the enemies. They were incredibly courageous, these little birds, and with all their bravery, they were guarding their nests. Without hesitation, without any fear, they were running at any size of the enemy, rushing into the battle for the protection of their offspring.

Alenushka often saw a very small bird fearlessly pursuing a crow or hawk many times bigger than the singing bird. Sometimes, two little birds were chasing their enemies, trying to peck their heads. But still, they need people to help them.

Crows

There were a lot of impudent crows on the ranch, and they were the most loathed vultures. When no one was around, insolent crows flew close to the house to bust songbird nests. Alenushka often saw how these greedy robbers, treacherous crows devastated someone's nests.. She always tried to scare them away from the trees, where singing birds made their nests. From their mistress her smart dogs were learning fast to react to the crows, as well.

German Shepard Tuzik periodically was expressing his concern about birds invading his front yard. Then he learned his new job in protecting the birds. He started to bark at the crows and hawks, warning Alenushka to come out with the gun. Sometimes the dogs looked up, saying: *"It is the time to do something drastically against these cocky crows."*

In the cowardly and indolent nature of the crows, it was customary to act out of the blue, out of cunning and meanness. When the mother of a singing bird flew for food for her chicks, the crows were right there, deceivingly flew to the unprotected nests and attacked the tender chicks. When Alenushka heard the loud noise of the hunting crows, she fast was coming out of the house with a gun to scare them. The ill-mannered crows, yelling in a nasty hoarse voice, were afraid of the loud screams or waved hands of people, and always flew away.

Crows and Hawk

While living on the ranch, Alenushka observed that every animal brought its own benefit to nature or was serving for something. One was a predator and hunted for someone. The other was someone's prey. It was a natural circle of life.

There were many tall palms trees along the western road. Victusha planted them many years ago to protect his avocado trees from the strong setting sun. At the end of this road, there was a hawk's nest high on the last tree. There were many of them were breeding in recent years around the ranch.

The owner of the ranch Victusha was happy about that because they were cleaning the area from the rats, squirrels, and other small animals. But Alenushka did not like these strong predators. Especially one of them bothered her a lot, when he loudly and heavily shouted during the hunt, disturbing her soul.

The hawks had a more bold personality than the crows, and flew very close to the house, ravaged the nests of songbirds, and eating the chicks. They were not afraid of either shot or screaming people.

One spring, Alenushka and her dogs Tuzik and Sonya were walking on the western road. From a distance, they already saw that the crows flew in a huge flock to the high palm tree, where the Hawk's nest was. The aggressive crows worked as a team and made horrific and greedy noise of hunting.

Several crows were sitting on the palm tree near the hawk nest, looking as if a hawk was coming to protect his chicks. And at the same time, other crows have been eating everything in the nest. Then they changed their roles.

While the hawk-parent was hunting for some food for its chicks, his babies were thrown to the mercy of their fate. They were helpless in the absence of their parents.

This time Alenushka did not want that the crows would take advantage of the unprotected chicks in the Hawk's Nest. She and her loyal dogs ran to the palm tree together, shouting and waving their arms, trying to scare off the crows. But it was too late. When the Hawk arrived, there was nothing in the nest. The Hawk sat on a branch near the destroyed nest, holding food in its beak. He turned around his head, looking for the enemies. After this incident, the Hawk settled further and higher on a nearby mountain among the neighbor's avocado plantations.

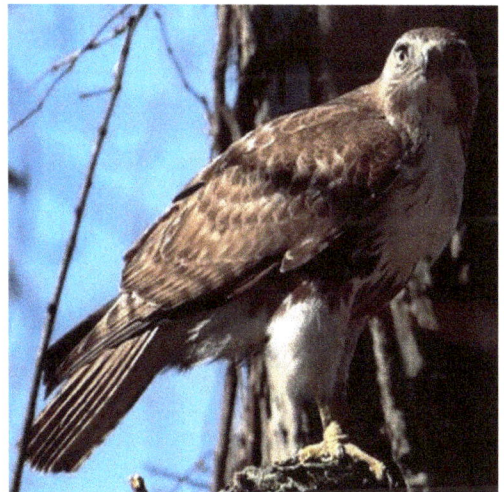

Bird-Parent lessons

Different birds have diverse voices and diverse characters. Some sing loudly and talk to each other during activities throughout the day. Others are more quiet and private, hiding between the branches of the garden trees. Many birds have a tradition, that the father is providing the food for the babies.

One Spring Alenushka watched a bird family in the garden. They recently had a new son Bobby and were teaching him to get some food on his own. Every morning and before the sunset, they would come to the garden to get some food. Mother Bird immediately walked forward, far from her husband and away from her adorable, but a little noisy, son. She liked to enjoy her breakfast alone, in peace and solitude.

But her husband was not as lucky as she was, and he could not have one peaceful meal. Their son was always hungry, and the good father felt obligated to feed him. The bird Bobby already was almost the same size as his parents, but he does not want to do anything for himself. He was running near his father's side, with a wide-open mouth. When he saw that his father got something from under the grass, Bobby immediately pushed his open mouth to his father's beak. He constantly and very loudly demanding: "*Give me more food! Give me more*!"

It looked like the hard-working father did not have any time to eat. He was making a strong effort to teach his son Bobby to get the food and live independently. Once, Bobby-bird looked down without searching for the food just to demonstrate that he did what his father told him to do. He did not find anything, gave up, and continued to run after his father with his widely opened mouth.

Then, several different birds came, looked at this annoying scene, disapproved it, and escaped fast on their own business.

Every morning Alenushka recognized the distinguished voice of the Bobby-bird and watched the same scene. But in several days, the father changed his techniques. When he saw some food down in the grass, he would stop near it, waiting when his son would come closer. Then, the smart father would run away from his hungry and unskilled son. But Bobby kept running after the father, demanding the food, instead of looking down and finding the seeds in the grass.

Once, his mother came close to them and watched it for a while. But she was annoyed by the yelling and demanding voice of the baby bird. Then, she quickly jumped between the baby and his father and pushed the boy away. The baby bird was shocked by that action of his mother, stood for a moment with no yelling.

On the next day Father-bird tried a new teaching tactic. He found something in the grass and took it in his mouth. Then, instead of giving it to his son, the father was

just holding the delicious snack in his own mouth, looking in a different direction. Instead, the father suddenly swallowed it and began to run away, yelling back: *"Try again to find the food, my son. All food is under your feet, just look for it!"* Bobby-bird did not have any other choice, but to pick up some food by himself. His father taught him a good lesson.

On the next morning after breakfast, Baby bird and his parents had a family meeting. With joy and excitement, they stated, that their son had gained the skills of food finding.

Now they had a different agenda, to teach their son some social skills. His parents discussed it with big excitement. Suddenly, Bobby-bird said: *"I will be happy to learn how to fit well in the bird community."* The parents stopped talking for a while from this unexpectedly mature statement of their son.

Then Father said: *"God gave you parents. But you will be making friends by your own choice. Your purpose is to keep them for a lifetime."* And his Mother added: *"We are happy only when we have someone to share our happiness with. The more you would share, - the more joy you will get back, and the happier you will be."* With these wise thoughts, they let Bobby alone to live independently. The Bobby-bird learned that in order to succeed in any society, it was important to be pleasant to everybody around.

On the closest tree, Alenushka saw one family of birds who was singing their glory to the new and beautiful day. She watched them for a while, and then went on her own human life.

Baby Owl

One evening Alenushka and her dogs were walking before bedtime. Suddenly, the dogs got very excited, especially the big dog Tuzik. He even tried to jump up and climb on the palm tree. Alenushka came closer and saw a very unusual animal, sitting upside down on the trunk of the palm tree. When Victusha came he recognized that it was a baby owl.

For the baby Owl, it was the first night out from the mother's nest, and he did not know what to do with his wings. The baby Owl stuck on the trunk of the palm tree and did not have any strength to move anymore. The voice of his mother was nearby, encouraging him to fly to her. The baby Owl breathed heavily and was opening his mouth trying to tell her that he does not have any strength even to talk. But no sound came out of his mouth.

Alenushka had never seen such a small baby Owl and wanted to help him. Therefore, she locked dogs in the front yard, where they continued to have their excitement. Then, she went to the house and brought a long, soft, and fluffy duster brush. Victusha handed the soft end of the stick towards the baby Owl. The bird immediately grabbed it, again hanging upside down on it.

The baby Owl was very cute and puffy, but he did not know how to fly and knew nothing about the world around him. Victusha took the bird to his truck, where the little Owl laid down, felt safer. However, his mother was very upset that the people were interfering with her own business of teaching her baby to fly. She was nervously flying around, called her

baby, still persuading her son to try to fly harder.

Alenushka went back to the yard to get some water for the bird. But when she came back, the bird was gone. So, the baby Owl learned a little about how to use his big wings. However, Alenushka was afraid that the bird might fell down close by and coyotes would get it. She asked Victusha to walk around with the strong flashlight, looking for the Baby Owl. Soon, they found the owl, who was quietly sitting on the edge of the road, looking at the people with big innocent eyes.

Victusha said: "*Let's the nature would take its course.*"

And they went back home. But later at night, Alenushka still was worry about the bird and went to see what's happened. His mother's voice sounded nearby, and she still was teaching him how to fly.

Next Night

One old and observant Hawk long ago noticed that local Owls nested on the western side of the hill near the house. But only at sunrise and sunset did the Owls fly out of their hiding place to hunt or teach their children. At that time, the smart and always hungry Hawk also often would come to the western side of the hill. He would circle there, waiting for the Owl or its cubs to appear.

Alenushka was happily hearing how the Owl father was teaching his cub to hoot as all Owls should do. First, the father Owl was doing it loudly and confidently, and then, he told his baby to repeat it after him. But the cub just mumbled back something silly in his thin and tender voice. Their voices were clearly audible in the night.

Nearby, a happy voice of a young mother Owl was replying to them with her approval and joy. The owl mother was sitting a little further from the baby, letting the father have the opportunity to express his love for their cub. Only occasionally she sent them her approval and her enthusiasm for the new successes of her son. The father-Owl brought a mouse to the nestling, and the baby-owl was still enjoying a free breakfast in the parent's house. Then, the Owl father taught his son a hunting lesson.

The rare happiness and peace reigned in this night.

But how long such serene happiness would reign on the ranch? How much time the happy Owl family would live in the wild nature with no troubles or fights for the surviving?

***

Sky King - Hawk

The parents-owls were so much involved in teaching their son that they did not notice that the night is over. The safe, comfortable dark night was their friend, but it was already gone. With the rising sun, the danger of the daylight came for the owls.

Alenushka and her dogs were walking on the West road, thinking that the baby-owl continues to comprehend the basics of the wildlife. Suddenly, from the side of the last palm tree, where there was a hawk's nest, a terrifying, warlike cry started.

Alenushka looked up and saw a huge hawk was rushing to the place where the father-owl was sitting with the chick. Alenushka tried to scare away that hawk, but he did not pay any attention to her waving hands and loud but helpless yells. At the same time, but a little further, she heard a warning, excited cry of an owl-mother. The Owl-father tried to protect his little baby as courageously as he could…

The next night, walking before bedtime with dogs, no one heard the happy scream of an owl, the babbling of its new cubs, or the hoot of the father - owl. Over the ranch was a sad silence.

First several days, the survived owl was searching for her friend. She flew from one tree to another tree, visiting the places where they spent their happy time. She loudly, in a dreary voice, desperately called him. Then, the next night, the Owl flew onto the roof of the house, where they often happily met before on the moonlight nights. She screamed for a long time, with longing and despair. No one responded to her call.

Alenushka understood well the language of many animals. After a long time living on a ranch, she learned to understand the language of birds, as well. One night she got up, walked outside, and said to the owl:"*If you find a friend, settle closer to the house. I will try to protect you from the hawks*".

Then, for the next several days, the Owl was silent. Then, for several days she again flew from tree to tree, calling for her friend. And suddenly, a miracle happened, and her new friend flew to her. Life was in a circle of eternity and life was going on...

But after this incident, Alenushka walked everywhere with her gun, trying to scare away the hawks and crows or get revenge for the gentle owls.

***

One of the hawks was no longer young, and now very smart and observant. Soon he realized that on the palm trees near the house various songbirds were building nests

and raising tasty chicks. Especially gullible pigeons, which always lived in loving pairs, were very easy prey for the fast Hawk.

Sometimes they sat on the fence, looking around with curiosity and gently, quietly cooing. Although most of the day, they hid under the shady trees of the garden, sometimes they flew out into the open area or sat on the wide road leading to the house.

Pairs of pigeons roamed along that road picking up seeds, and took off only at the last moment when a cat, a car, or a dog was rushing very close towards them. The swift hawk dived down with a wild cry and bit off the small pigeon's head. Then, at the same great speed, he immediately, in a hurry, flew back.

***

One day Alenushka with Victusha and their dogs Tuzik and Sonya walked along the western road near the palm trees. Suddenly they saw the Hawk circling high in the sky. Alenushka immediately began to run back and forth, waving her jacket and shouting loudly at the Hawk. The dogs became agitated, began to jump, and even tried to take off.

The hawk was very surprised at such annoying noise and such an unexpected hindrance to his hunt. He began to circle lower and lower, descending closer and closer to Alenushka and her dogs. Hawk easily could grab a rabbit, a duck or a cat and take it away to his nest. Only snakes were often daring to get away from the Hawk.

Getting down to the ground, this Hawk obviously was estimating if he could get one of the dogs, Sonia or Tuzik, as his meal. But the dogs were German Shepherds--too big for a Hawk.

However, the Hawk was clearly surprised that anyone at all had the courage to shout something angrily at him or to indicate how and where he should hunt. The hawks are not used to this. They do not have such daredevils in nature who would threaten them. The Hawk went down so low that Alenushka saw his sharp eyes, all-seeing at long distances. The hawk examined everyone below on the ground and laughed venomously. It was clear and understandable to him that nothing threatened his hunt. But the sun had already set below the horizon and painted the west in bright colors. The Hawk flapped his wings and flew off to the distant mountain. Apparently, he still decided that it was better not to risk it and stay away from such loud dogs, and people waving their arms and jackets. After that and for a long time, Alenushka did not see this Hawk on the western side of the ranch.

***

Interesting

California hosts an amazing diversity of birds. It is a key link along the Pacific Flyway, the migratory route traveled by millions of birds every year.

The most common backyard birds throughout the year in California: House Finch, Black Phoebe, Anna's Hummingbird, American Crow, Mourning Dove, California Scrub-Jay, White-crowned Sparrow, Dark-eyed Junco, California Towhee, Oak Titmouse, Cedar Waxwing, Cooper's Hawk, and others.

It is good if a child could have a space to explore and feel connected to the natural world.

***

Owls are amazing birds. They form monogamous pairs, and settle only in pairs. Pairs of owls do not build their nests. They occupy crevices, hollows, or nests abandoned by other birds. Owls can breed one or several times a year, it all depends on the amount of food in the habitat. In a clutch there can be from 3 to 10 eggs. The female owl incubates eggs. A male owl is involved in feeding offspring. It is that different ages of birds live in the same nest. The parents feed all offspring, but priority is given to the oldest babies.

Owls are quite useful for the environment, because they destroy many harmful rodents. But owls never eat carrion. For the winter period, they make stocks and store them directly in the nest. The digestive system of this bird is designed so that they need to eat a whole carcass of the mouse.

In Egypt, owls were treated with respect and even mummified. It is believed that owls were guards or companions of goddesses. In Christianity Owl symbolized desolation, loneliness, sorrow and solitude. For the ancient Slavonic cultures, the owl was the keeper of underground treasures, and foreshadowed fire or death. In addition to the mystical symbol, the owl has always been a symbol of mind and wisdom.

Color These Birds

***

The eagle does not catch flies

***

The hen flies not far unless the cock flies with her

***

The seagull sees farthest who flies highest

***

A fine cage won't feed the bird

***

The owl sees in his son a falcon

***

A bird does not sing because it has an answer

***

What's good for the goose is good for the gander

***

The chicken that cries at night will not lay eggs in the morning

***

Live with vultures, become a vulture; live with crows, become a crow

***

God loved the birds and invented trees

***

People live like birds in the woods: When the time comes, each must take flight

***

The sky is wide enough for two birds to fly without their wings touching.

***

DOVE

CROW

CRANE

HUMMINGBIRD

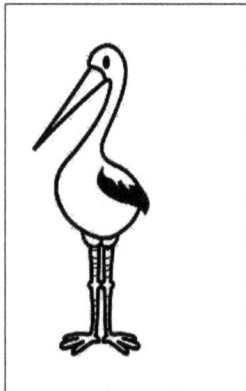
STORK- CAPTAIN

LOVING SWANS

Birds of a feather flock together

***

A bird never flew on one wing

***

The early bird catches the worm, but it is the early worm that gets caught

***

A bird in the hand is worth two in the bush

***

The falcon does not struggle when he is caught

***

Even an eagle will not fly higher than the sun

***

God gives all birds their food but does not drop it into their nests

***

OWL

TITMOUSE

COOKATOO

EAGLE

PARROT

DUBONOS

SCREAMIN G OWL

KARAKARA

SWAN (BLACK SWAN)

CROW

 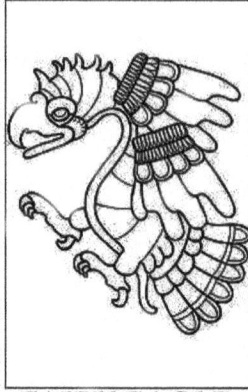   

| SWAN | FAIRY EAGLE | | | SIRIN |

| PHOENIX | BIRD of HAPPINESS | PINK FLAMINGO | | HAWK |

***

You cannot stop birds from flying over your head, but you can stop them nesting in your hair.

***

Rights Reserved

***

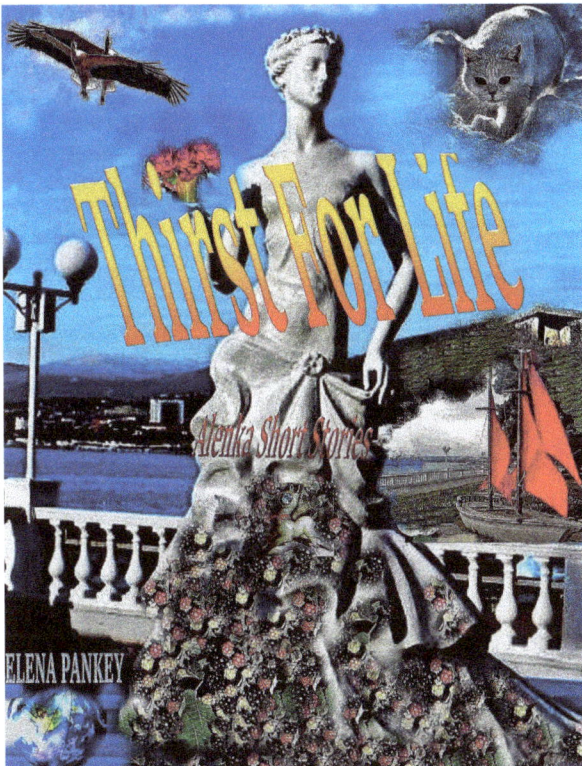

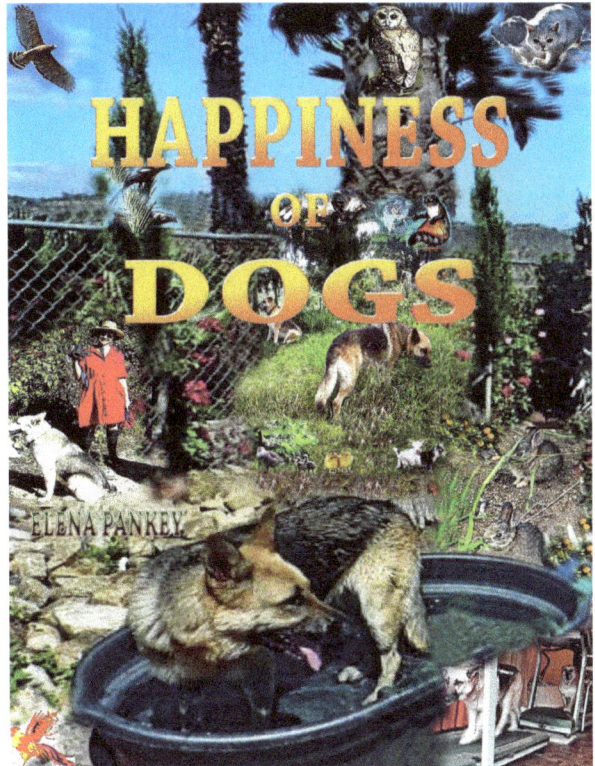

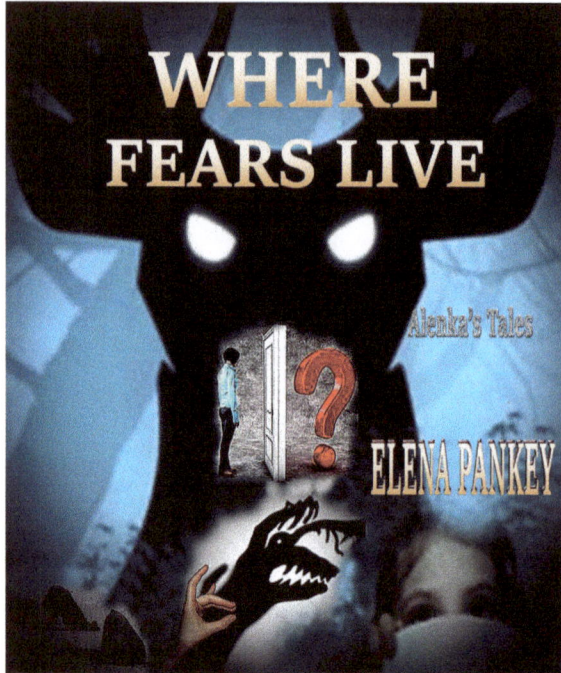

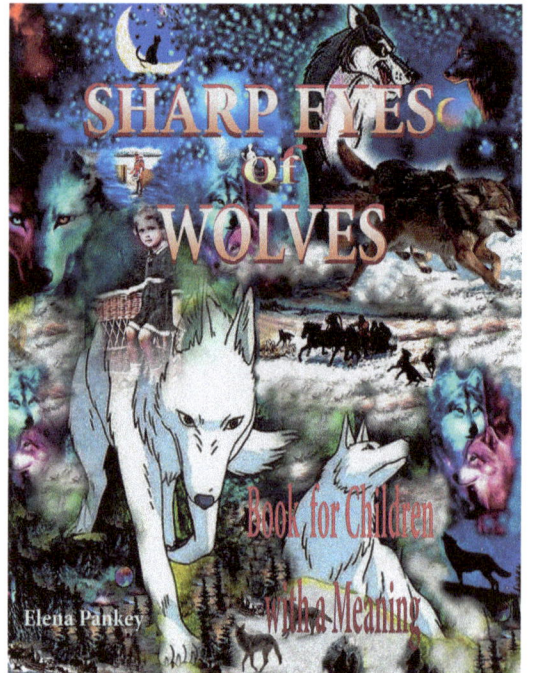

978-1-952907-50-0

***

www.ingramcontent.com/pod-product-compliance
Lightning Source LLC
Chambersburg PA
CBHW042337030426
42335CB00028B/3369